*The Coach's Guide to*

# REAL WINNING

## Teaching Life Lessons to Kids in Sports

## JOHN L. SHANNON, JR.

Addicus Books
Omaha, Nebraska

ISBN# 1-886039-56-9
*Cover design by Peri Poloni*
*Ilustrations by Jack Kusler*
*Typography by Linda Dageforde*

**Library of Congress Cataloging-in-Publication Data**

Shannon, John L., 1953-
    The coach's guide to real winning! : teaching life lessons to kids in
sports / John L. Shannon, Jr.
       p. cm.
"An Addicus nonfiction book."
    ISBN 1-886039-56-9 (alk. paper)
    1. Sports for children—Coaching. I. Title.
    GV709.24 .S52 2000
    796'.07'7—dc21                       2001001492

Addicus Books, Inc.
P.O. Box 45327
Omaha, Nebraska 68145
Web site: www.AddicusBooks.com

Printed in the United States of America
10 9 8 7 6 5 4 3 2 1

*To my lovely bride Katy and
to my three "winning" sons, Cory, Brady, and Case*

# Contents

# Acknowledgments

I would like to express my gratitude and affection to Leo Goslin, my high school football and hockey coach. Coach Goslin taught me how much fun competition and hard work is. His influence is the single greatest reason why I pursued an undergraduate degree in secondary education with hopes of coaching high school sports.

I would also like to thank Jerry Noyce, my former coach of the University of Minnesota tennis team and Division I National Tennis Coach of the Year. Jerry built a tennis franchise in Minnesota by his leadership on and off the court, and I will always be indebted to him for giving me the opportunity to enjoy a "perfect" career.

I would be remiss if I did not acknowledge the finest teaching tennis professional in the country, Frank Voigt. I had the great pleasure of working with Frank for many years. Always the consummate gentleman, Frank treated everyone with dignity. And, he taught me the importance of learning how to teach each individual differently. Frank is no longer with us, but remains an indelible memory to all those whose lives he touched. One of my luckiest breaks in life was to work with this truly outstanding individual.

I am also grateful to the many wonderful men and women I have coached with throughout the years in community youth athletic programs. They are too numerous to list here, but I would like to mention Kevin Dulin, no one is more professional or prepared; Dick Lewis, no one is more committed; Kevin Johnson, no one is worthier of more respect; and Mark Heyne, who always has his heart in the right spot. I also thank Brad "Cookie" Carlson; no one created more fun or had more fun than he.

Finally, I must acknowledge my "life coach," my father Jack. Always constant in purpose and deed, he has demonstrated integrity and service in every aspect of life, and positively affects everyone he meets. I am so proud to call him Dad.

# Introduction

*A man never stands as tall as when he kneels to help a child.*
—Knights of Pythagoras

Every year more than 4 million volunteer coaches work with over 40 million young athletes in the United States, according to the Positive Coaching Alliance. Many of these adults have never coached before, and certainly most have never received formal training in working with young children in an athletic setting. It is my hope that *Real Winning— Teaching Life Lessons to Kids in Sports* will serve as an inspirational guide for all the generous volunteer coaches in community athletic programs who work with children ages five to fifteen.

During the past thirty years, I have worked with many kids and experimented with different approaches to coaching. I have also observed many other coaches. Unfortunately, an increasing number of coaches today exhibit an unhealthy level of intensity that rivals college and professional levels of competition. These overzealous coaches berate players, officials, and other coaches. They also limit playing time to only the very best players in hopes of pulling in a big "W."

Virtually every time I talk to these coaches about their teams, the conversation inevitably turns to their win/loss records. If they are winning, they light up with pride. If they are losing, they describe their players as weak or as having behavior problems. Some of these coaches approach the season with a "win at any cost" mind-set. Although some will have a winning season, they will also lose many players in the process. Rarely do I hear these coaches talk about the improvement of their teams—as players, as units, and as individuals.

Coaches must focus on lessons that go far beyond the field of competition. If we are to be truly "winning coaches," we must help kids develop character and integrity—qualities that will forever enrich their lives. This is real winning.

We coaches today are in a prime position to help our kids grow. Our influence on children is not fleeting. It lasts a lifetime.

*They may forget what you said,*
*but they will never forget how you made them feel.*
—Carl W. Buechner

# Part I

## What "Winning Coaches" Know

*Children are the living messages we send to a time we will not see.*
—John W. Whitehead

# It's about the kids!

A "winning coach" becomes involved in coaching because he or she loves to watch kids play and grow. He or she measures the success of a season not by the number of games won, but by the number of "kids won"—those who are learning lessons that will make them winners in life. A "winning coach" knows that to help build "winning kids," he or she must first "win over" every child on the team. Enthusiastically, a "winning coach" invests one of his or her most precious gifts, time, in our most precious asset, our children.

# The child comes first, then the athlete, and then the sport.

A number of years ago, one of the parents of a boy on my hockey team asked me what my coaching priorities were. I had not given much thought to a question like this, so I didn't really have a prepared thought. But I thought for a moment and told her that my priorities were first, to assist in the development of a young person; second, to assist in the development of a young athlete; and lastly, to assist in the development of a young hockey player.

When I got home that evening, I wrote down a priority list on a piece of paper and put it in a new folder labeled Coaching. Through the years, I have added many thoughts to this folder. And each year I review it for my own benefit. In this whole collection of ideas, no one thought stands out to me more profoundly than my list of coaching priorities.

As coaches, we must remember this very simple priority: We are dealing with children first and foremost, then athletes and players. When we don't recall this fact, we risk ignoring the primary needs of the vast majority of the children with whom we work, children so urgently in need of our care and support.

# Assist in the development of a young person.

Most of the children we work with in a season will not play the sport(s) we coach in high school, let alone in college or beyond. They will not be the stars of their teams. They will be kids who play for a few years and then move on to other interests. What, then, should be our first priority? Simple. Our first priority should be to assist in their development as people, with an emphasis on teaching them life lessons.

As coaches, we need to give children on our teams the opportunity to experience situations that enhance their character and their future. The truly important ingredients for success in life don't have anything to do with goals, strikeouts, touchdowns, or free throws. They have everything to do with integrity, hard work, perseverance, teamwork, and the ability to deal with both adversity and success.

Not every kid we work with will be a great athlete, but our goal should be to assist every kid we work with to be a great person, one who makes great personal decisions.

If every youth athletic coach measures his or her success based on this criterion, each can strive for a "perfect season."

# Assist in the development of a physically fit youth.

Considering the increasingly sedentary lifestyle that many live and the health risks associated with it, we need to do everything possible to encourage children to make a life-long commitment to good health. All of us can encourage children to live a healthier life-style by modeling proper exercise, diet, and behavior. As coaches, we can give children a head start by helping build their physical assets of coordination, strength, balance, and conditioning. We need to be creative and structure our practices to build upon the basic building blocks of athleticism.

What we don't need to do is "turn off" a kid to a sport because he or she may be overweight or less gifted athletically. Too many times, these children are left behind by coaches because they may be less able to do what other children do, and therefore, may actually detract from the team's ability to win. These kids are the most important ones to keep actively involved. The positive experience a coach can give these less athletically gifted children may change their lives forever, for the better.

We need to build young athletes for their future as adults—adults who love to exercise and stay active because they can associate positive memories with these activities. That's a goal every coach can shoot for!

# Assist in the development of a young player of a specific sport.

With the first two priorities firmly in mind, our third priority is to teach our young athletes a specific sport—hockey, baseball, football, swimming, soccer, volleyball, basketball, you name it.

Coach, kids have been pestering their parents to sign them up to play your sport. Depending on the age and skill level of the child, parents have expectations ranging from simply introducing their young child to a sport to seeing a significant improvement in their child's skill level and understanding of the game. Now your job, as the parents see it, is to "give them their money's worth."

To meet expectations and optimize the potential for success, I strongly suggest putting together a plan. To me, a plan means a written outline for the entire season, one that specifically lists the kinds of activities that you will use to teach. Keeping the age and skill level in mind, develop your coaching objectives and put together a coaching calendar for the season in writing. The idea is to build the season for the kids and develop a rhythm and flow of learning. For example, if you have four weeks before your first game, develop a series of building blocks that will allow you to be prepared to compete. With younger children, this four-week period may be devoted primarily to instructing and fine-tuning technique, in such activities as throwing, shooting, skating, and passing. For an advanced team, this time may be best used to review basic skills. Early on, focus more on conditioning and styles of play the team will use. Later in the season, your coaching calendar will allocate time to explore the nuances of your sport so kids can move along the experience curve, maintain interest, and build confidence.

Failing to create and follow a plan may result in less than optimal results for your players, and may put them at a competitive disadvantage in years to come.

# Never forget that "sport" is defined as any athletic activity giving enjoyment or recreation.

The definition of "sports" does not involve any reference to winning or losing. To understand how a child views "sports," you don't have to go any further than watching a puppy. A puppy runs for the sheer pleasure of running. Put a group of puppies together and watch them play tag and wrestle, merely for the joy of exerting energy and competition.

If, as a coach, you extract the enjoyment from the athletic activity because of your intensity, then it's no longer a sport to a child. It becomes drudgery and a burden, and not too many kids are going to grow from the experience.

Take pleasure in watching kids run, exercise, and grow. Trust me, those are the memories you'll retain in your later years.

# Trust: the first building block for winning coaching.

The single most important ingredient for building a strong coaching relationship with a child is trust. Loosely defined, trust means that child knows and truly believes that you have his or her best interests at heart. At the beginning of the season and consistently throughout the year, you must convince each child on your team that you care about him or her as a person.

How do you accomplish this? Frankly, you have to put on your sales hat. It is your job to sell each child on your sincerity, your values, and what you see your purpose as coach to be. You look each of them in the eye when you speak. You are empathetic and tender with the players on your team.

At our very first practice of the year, I collect the kids around me and talk to them about my rules and our objectives for the season. Much of what is in this book, I share with them at the beginning—the importance of learning, working hard, getting better, and having fun; the emphasis on controllables versus uncontrollables; and the importance to use this season to assist in their "growing up."

Telling kids up front what you want for every player on your team during the season is a great first step to establishing and building upon their trust. But be careful. Kids have great memories. Don't promise something at the beginning of the season that you can't deliver.

# Remember who you are not!

You are not Vince Lombardi! This is not the NFL, or Notre Dame. You are not coaching a professional sports team! Your ego, athletic prowess, or coaching ability is not on the line. Your job is not on the line. Lighten up!

I am still dumbstruck at the seriousness, intensity, anger, and competitiveness that youth athletic coaches display on the sidelines. I recently witnessed a seventh grade football game. One of the assistant coaches was screaming at a kid to hustle off the field. Apparently, the twelve-year-old was not moving fast enough, so the coach grabbed him by the shoulder pads and yanked him to the sidelines, nearly throwing the youngster to the ground. One would have thought we were watching a professional football game with a league championship on the line. I am convinced that when he looked back on the incident, the coach realized how silly he looked, how humiliated he made his player feel, and how angry the player's parents were. But it's too late. The damage has been done.

Remember who you are. You're a volunteer coach who is there, first and foremost, to make a real difference in children's lives. Leave the histrionics behind.

# "Winning coaches" always remember that they are not playing the game.

It's a kid's game, played by kids for the benefit of kids. You are not a participant on the field of competition. When your team loses, that doesn't mean you personally lost, that you're a lousy coach, or that you won't be asked back next year. Similarly, if your team wins, that doesn't necessarily qualify you for the Coach of the Year award. Yet most coaches fall victim to the short-term euphoria and self-gratification of a "win."

"Winning coaches" have learned to keep their own competitive energies with respect to winning in check when coaching youth athletics. Sure, the kids want to see you care, and you want to see them win! But when a coach puts his personal need to win above the interests of all the players on the team, he has broken a contract with his players and failed his duty.

A few years ago one of my sons participated in a spring hockey league. For the first two games, he was placed as a substitute on the third line, and decisions were made during the games that resulted in virtually no playing time for him. His team won both games with the first line scoring all the goals and playing the majority of the time. My son lost interest in the sport and hung up his skates for a couple of years. My sense is, these coaches were personally competing, enjoyed coaching a "winning" team, and would do whatever was necessary not to lose. The fact that they "lost" a kid, one who thoroughly understood how they felt about him as a player, was an acceptable cost of having a winning team.

Don't make this mistake. I guarantee that you will make better decisions as a coach if you always remember that you are not playing the game!

# Build players' self-esteem to strengthen their positive decision-making ability.

Think about it. Is the score of the game, or how many games we win during a youth athletic season, really that important?

The really important "score" we should focus on is the number of great decisions our youngsters make in the future. Take it from me, these children grow up fast. Before you know it, they will start playing truly life-altering "games." Instead of taking place on courts and fields, these games will be played in new venues—basements, bedrooms, and the streets. Instead of decisions involving blocking and tackling, these decisions will involve drugs, sex, cigarettes, violence, and other life-altering behaviors. Every single one of our kids, from the star of the team to the child who needs the most help, will face these decisions in the very near future.

Our ultimate goal as coaches, and as a society, is to help prepare these kids to make the right decisions. Let's do everything we can to help them like themselves, care about themselves, and be strong enough to make the tough decisions they know are right.

# Do as I do!

Never forget that you are a role model every second that you are with a child! Your kids see everything you do, especially in times of crisis. It doesn't mean you have to be perfect; it just means that you must always be aware you are constantly teaching them and need to do your very best.

Don't tell the kids to be respectful to referees and then yell at them yourself, or make disparaging comments about refs in the kids' presence! Don't tell the kids to handle losing positively and then get uptight and angry, if you're on the wrong end of the score! Don't tell them to treat their bodies with care and then exhibit unhealthy behavior, such as drinking or smoking, in their presence. Kids are brilliant at spotting hypocrisy.

You teach children how to communicate by how you communicate with them. They will learn more from what you do than they ever will from what you say. As Ralph Waldo Emerson said, "What you do speaks so loudly that I cannot hear what you say."

# Remember why you were "hired."

True story. A few years back, the volunteer coach of a twelve-year-old boys soccer team told me he felt he "was hired to produce a team with a winning record." And that may have been the case. But Coach, the fact is, you were "hired" to teach these kids about hard work, discipline, courtesy, respect, and teamwork, in addition to soccer skills and knowledge. If you end up this year with a winning record, it will simply be a by-product of your success in all these areas and the quality of your schedule. By the way, if you turn out hardworking, mature young men who are significantly better soccer players at the end of the season and you don't win a single game, you've successfully met your job description.

Coaches, at the beginning of the season before your first practice, write down what you think your job description should be. You haven't seen any of the competition yet. You don't know how good your team really is. Jot down what you think your job is. And if you ever doubt during the year whether you're living up to the job specifications, pull it out and take a look. If you've been true to your convictions, win or lose, you're going to be satisfied you are doing your job!

# Don't ever underestimate the impact
# you have on children's lives.

You are not the most important person in the life of each member of your team. But don't kid yourself, you do leave an indelible mark on each child. As a coach, you join all the other members of your community who serve our youth and become vital threads in the fabric of their character. You are an important member of the "village" that raises a child.

We are seeing more and more kids from single-parent homes, split-parent homes, and some from difficult family situations. For the extremely brief period of time you spend coaching during a season, you may become the mother or father figure for some of the kids on your team. The hours they spend with you during practices or at games may be the times they look most forward to all week. That's a big responsibility. Don't treat it lightly!

Remember, children can never have too many positive adult role models in their lives. Never!

# Keep 'em coming back!

Instead of asking how many games you won last year, maybe we should ask: "Coach, how many kids from your team last year are playing your sport again this year?" Many youth coaches feel it's their duty to weed out members of their team who just aren't going to cut it in the future.

Remember, kids develop at different times. The slow-of-foot child today may be the speedster of tomorrow. The small of stature today may be the basketball center tomorrow. And the converse is true. I have no idea if that slow, small, tentative kid on your eleven-year-old's team will ever be a contributor to the high school team one day, but I know with certainty that he won't be a contributor if a coach chases him out of the sport prematurely. I remember hearing a high school coach say, "Boy, I wish Ryan was playing basketball now." But I knew Ryan, now six feet five, had given the sport up years ago because he was spoken to so roughly by his coach and was given very limited playing time.

Even if some members of your team aren't going to become even mediocre in terms of performance, your job is to coach your team in a way that makes it fun for every player to come back next year. Don't ever allow yourself to think of prematurely forcing a kid out of a community sports program because you, in your infinite wisdom, don't think he or she has what it takes.

We want kids to participate in sports for as long as they want to. Virtually every study of adolescents suggests that engaging in sports is an indicator of success in high school and is associated with a healthier lifestyle. Trust me, it's in everyone's best interest to keep children involved in healthy activities like athletics for as long as we can.

# Unorganized sports are where players flourish!

Could it be that today our children's lives are too organized? Our children seem busier than ever. Sadly, I think many parents today don't feel comfortable with their kids riding their bikes to the park and spending the day just exploring without adult supervision. We yearn for the safety of organized activities. But there is a significant downside to organization. Our children are losing the gift of spontaneity, of just dropping everything and doing what they want to do in the moment. Also, they are losing the opportunity to learn (as we did) how to get along with each other, without parents and other adults around.

Today the coaching obsession with structured practices and "running drills" is stealing our children's ability to be creative and to develop individuality. I have a couple of ideas to help counter this tendency.

First, try to incorporate as many unorganized drills into your practices as possible. Organized drills involve activities such as, skating around cones, dribbling in lines, tackling blocking dummies, and batting. Unorganized drills are just that, drills that are structured to be more chaotic with fewer "right" things to do. Unorganized drills allow more freedom for players to hone their skills, to test their boundaries, to create, to improvise. A dad once came up to me after one of my hockey practices and said, "Coach, that was the most organized unorganized practice I've ever seen." Exactly!

Secondly, strongly encourage your kids to play your sport outside organized practices and games. In hockey, our kids get significantly better in January and February. That's also when they play unorganized pond hockey outdoors. Just a coincidence? Think again. We aren't teaching them. They are teaching themselves and each other!

# Girls and boys do not live by one sport alone!

Encourage your players to play many sports. You will find they will become better athletes and may avoid burnout.

My experience is that zealous coaches in one sport try to extend the season by promoting additional leagues. Winter league turns into spring league into summer league into fall league. Many experts share the concern that we are forcing sport specialization prematurely. Of course, a child may want to participate in a sport for an extended period of time. If so, the right questions to ask are "Is it good for him?" "What other things could she do with her time?" and "Should we be seeking more balance in the child's life?"

In addition, studies are now suggesting that kids who play many sports may be less prone to certain kinds of stress injuries as they age. These "kids" are going to be around for a long time, and they might as well be in good shape for as long as possible.

Coaches, go ahead and advocate other sporting activities for your players. Trust me, they'll come back to "your" sport more solid and enthusiastic athletes.

# Become a positive memory!

Whether as a significant memory, or just one of the many little memories associated with other positive adult role models in your community, you will become a part of each young person that you come in contact with as a coach.

I have three sons. When my two oldest sons turned sixteen, I sent them a little note with some fatherly advice. I closed each letter with the following: "When it's all said and done, a man has no more than his memories and his reputation. Live your life fully in a way that creates great memories—memories that you create for others, as well as for yourself! And live your life in a way that is consistent with your moral compass. You have a great deal of personal integrity—always be true to your inner sense. Throughout your life, have integrity in thought, purpose, and deed. If you follow your conscience, you will never lead you astray!"

"Winning coaches" create great memories for others, as well as for themselves.

# Part II

## Preseason Wisdom and Start-Up Tips

*A teacher affects eternity. He can never tell where his influence stops.*
—Henry Brooks Adams

# Hold a preseason meeting.

No matter how long or short your season, or what age group you are coaching, have a brief preseason meeting. Invite all players and parents, and try to make it mandatory for both groups. This meeting should be as professional as you can make it. (Standing in front of a group of parents and fumbling with a presentation at the beginning of the season doesn't exactly inspire confidence.) Have a packet of information, typed if possible, prepared for each family. Type up a player roster with all the parents' names, addresses, and phone numbers. It helps with carpooling and the like.

Before the meeting, try to anticipate the questions you might be asked and have the answers available. Typical questions will involve the game and practice scheduling, uniforms, pictures. Some may get into your coaching philosophy. Whether or not they ask about this latter subject, share your perspectives and expectations up front, with both players and parents. I can assure you that this will save misunderstandings and hassles later on!

This meeting is also an opportunity for you to create a positive relationship with the parents on your team. This will facilitate better communication throughout the season.

Lastly, get parents involved in the administration of your team. Delegate. You can't do it all by yourself. You will be a better coach if you delegate. Get a team parent, manager, or coordinator depending on the needs of your program. Good organization is essential to a successful season. Everyone has more fun when things are running smoothly.

# Everyone play your positions!

Sometimes I wonder if this generation of parents has become too actively involved in its kids' sports. Their involvement has become increasingly apparent on the sidelines of youth athletics today, with parents shouting instructions to their kids during games. You must deal with the parents up front and tell them what you expect. It is your expectation that all should play their positions: players should play, coaches should coach, referees should referee, and parents should be supportive fans!

Diplomatically tell your team parents not to "coach" their kids during a game. Let them know that doing so can cause several problems: parents may be giving instructions that are counter to those of the coaching staff; parents may force you, the coach, to compete with them for the attention of their child; and they may embarrass their child and the team.

I had one mom who literally ran up and down the sidelines shouting instructions to and cheering on her favorite player. Her son came up to me after the game and said, "She's embarrassing me, Coach." After a little coaxing, "Mom" was relatively inconspicuous during the rest of the season, and everybody on the team was happier. Cheering, offering positive comments, and otherwise showing enthusiasm are great tasks for parents during a game, and you can encourage this type of behavior. But let parents know that while they have a very important role in ensuring the success of the season, during a game, it's a limited role.

# Ask parents to support coaches and officials.

No question about it, parents play the most important role in creating respect for coaches and officials. At the beginning of the year, emphasize to your players' parents how important their support of authority figures is. Tell them up front that many people make mistakes during a game—players, coaches, even referees. But nobody is making a mistake on purpose, and the biggest mistake of all is to have parents demean an authority figure in front of their children.

As a coach, you can tell which parents support the authority figures in their child's life. When I was coaching tennis, I had a rule for my team: if you throw your racquet during a match, I will default you. A young, very talented player tested me early in the year. I defaulted him and almost cost our team the match. He never threw his racquet again. A few years later, I saw his dad at a tennis shop. He was telling me of his son's accomplishments at a military academy and brought up the racquet-throwing incident. He told me that was a big event in his son's life and thanked me. I said, "I appreciate the compliment, but I think it's misplaced. My sense is that when your son got into the car after that match, he complained to you about how unfair his coach was, and that you, in no uncertain terms, supported me. Am I right?" He grinned and nodded. The moral of the story? "Winning coaches" depend on parents to positively impact children's lives. If parents respect and support coaches and referees, they are teaching their kids to do so, too.

# Set the right season objectives: Learn, work hard, significantly improve, and have fun!

I believe it is essential that you, as a youth coach, put in writing what you want your kids to accomplish during the season and then hand it out to your players so they know what you want to accomplish. I have found that qualitative objectives are more meaningful and serve as better motivators for kids. Here are mine:

- Learn about: the basics, the game, strategy, teamwork, your teammates, and even more about yourself!
- Work hard! Nothing important was ever accomplished without hard work! Athletics and exercise are essential to live a long, successful life!
- Significantly improve as a person, an athlete, and a player in your sport!
- Have fun! If you accomplish these first three objectives, you're guaranteed to have fun!

I have used these objectives for every age group, from six-year-olds to four-teen-year-olds. They work for everyone, regardless of age, sport, skill level, or gender. Every single player on my team can internalize these objectives and make them his or her own. As the child matures and gets better, these objectives can remain the same—only the intensity and sophistication of attempting to achieve these objectives differ.

I have never liked establishing quantitative objectives for youth athletics—winning the division or getting to State. If you stay true to your qualitative objectives and have the talent that year and a favorable schedule, a quantitative objective may just take care of itself. But imagine if you do set a quantitative objective, such as "win our division," and don't reach it. Would you want your kids to see the season as a failure? I sure hope not!

# Be happy with who you've got on your team.

It's absolutely amazing to me to hear the carping from some youth coaches regarding what players they got "stuck" with. As far as I know, community sports programs don't involve recruitment efforts, draft choices, cash to bargain with, perks, or contracts to attract players to play on a certain team. I have always tried to take this attitude: "Just give me whomever the association wants me to have, and we'll have a ball developing young people, athletes, and a team." In the long run, the key isn't who you get—it's what you do for them!

And remember, unhappiness with whom we get "stuck" may run both ways. Some of the kids on your team may not be very happy to get you as their coach! Your challenge is to win them over, not the other way around.

I have coached for a number of years in a recreational soccer program held in the fall. One year we had so many kids sign up that we had to hold a coaches' meeting to divide the players in an attempt to make up equal teams. During a session to select fifth and sixth grade teams, one of my fellow coaches made a number of disparaging comments about the behavior of a sixth grade boy assigned to a team. The coach of this team was new to coaching, and she was afraid that she could not handle this child. I traded a player assigned to me in exchange for this "problem" child. Funny thing is, since I didn't know this child and didn't treat him as a problem kid, the two of us and our whole team had a ball that season. By the way, he was a heck of a soccer player!

# Attempt to create a competitive balance in each of your players.

You know this. Every single kid on your team is different. Some are innately competitive. These kids literally feel that their very existence hinges on the results of a game. They are your warriors. They will walk through fire for you in search of a win. Sometimes they are not only tough on themselves, but also vicious to their teammates. Some of your kids are innately passive. These children literally become spectators during a game. If you forgot to put them in the game during the last half, they may not even notice. Some may even attempt to remove themselves from a game because they don't think they are helping the team.

To optimize team play, I suggest trying to create a competitive balance in each of your players. For your warriors, who typically may ride an emotional roller coaster during games and practices, work on maintaining perspective with respect to winning and losing and exercising more self-control with their peers. For your passive players, be more inspiring with your direction, go out of your way to call on them more often, have them demonstrate drills, and most of all, give praise when a job is well done. "Winning coaches" are successful at bringing all types of personalities together as a cohesive unit.

But do realize you are not going to change the inherent personality of a child, nor should you try! You are there to positively influence the emotional center of the kids on your team, but children will grow and evolve in unique ways on their own.

# Kids love discipline.
## They just want to know the rules.

Virtually all child-care professionals will tell you that kids want boundaries—rules and discipline. Boundaries demonstrate that we care for them. Boundaries are important to reinforce personal discipline, responsibility, and accountability. Accordingly, it is mandatory at the beginning of the season that you communicate to your kids what the rules of behavior are, as well as the consequences of unacceptable behavior. Kids need to know that treating teammates, opponents, coaches, and referees with respect is mandatory. They need to know when to listen and when to speak. They need to know that swearing, yelling, and hitting will not be tolerated. First, set the rules. Then consistently and fairly enforce these rules, particularly if it's your son or daughter who is misbehaving.

One year I had a great soccer team of eight-year-olds. After a very close and surprisingly physical game, two of my players refused to shake the hands of the other team. I pulled the two of them aside and firmly, but appropriately, explained that they had both broken one of our rules. They both stuttered around a bit and offered some weak retorts.

Finally one of them said, "Coach, you're pretty tough on us with these rules of yours, don't you think?" I thought for a minute, and responded, "Well, I guess you're right. I am pretty tough when it comes to enforcing our rules." Then I looked him straight in the eyes, smiled, and asked, "Is it OK that I'm tough on you?" It took him a second and he smiled back, a big smile, and said, "Yeah, it's OK…In fact, I guess I like it." Setting boundaries is no more than paving a wide path to success for our children.

# Kids have two time clocks.

It's a quirk of nature. From my perspective, children are born with two internal time clocks. For coaches, this phenomenon is most pronounced during a game. The first clock is running when a child is playing in the game. The second clock takes over when the child is sitting on the bench waiting to go into the game.

When the child is on the first clock, every minute he or she plays seems like ten seconds. The kid plays for half an hour and it feels as if it's been only a few minutes. However, when the child is sitting on the bench waiting to play, every minute feels like an hour.

It may save you some long faces on the bench during the season if you tell them up front about this phenomenon. And don't get too frustrated yourself when one or two players on your team always asks, "Can I go in now, Coach?"

# Part III

## Practicing and Playing the Game

*We worry about what a child will become tomorrow,*
*yet we forget that he is someone today.*
—Stacia Tauscher

# Everyone should be having a ball, especially you!

Coach, you be the leader on this front. You have fun! Smile! Get excited! Be funny! Exude energy! Sports are supposed to be fun! Is there anything better than the privilege of running around with a group of enthusiastic young athletes? Not for me!

I have had my share of difficult business dealings through the years. I can honestly say that it has never taken more than five minutes with these kids to forget about the problems at the office. Get caught up in the euphoria of youth! It's downright therapeutic!

And don't kid yourself. The children on your team will know if you are having fun. The simple truth is, having fun is contagious! If you're having fun, the kids will too. So, enjoy and have a ball!

# Be prepared in writing for every practice and game.

Never come to practice without a well thought-out, written "lesson" plan with clear objectives in mind and a detailed schedule to optimize learning, participation, and fun. You have only a limited time with these kids each week, and you've got a lot to do in just a little bit of time. Take the time to put down on paper what you plan to do in time increments. This doesn't mean that you have to be a drillmaster for the entire practice. You can and should set aside time for fun and "unorganized" activities. If you take the time to write up a lesson plan, I guarantee you'll be more effective, and the preparation will not be lost on the parents and the kids.

This is true for games as well. Before every game, set up in writing playing time to ensure that each player gets a fair share of playing time and position. If you don't do this beforehand, you risk getting too involved in the game and denying some players the opportunity to contribute to the team. Putting it in writing also increases the level of your commitment to live up to your game plan, even when the game gets a little too close for comfort.

# The younger, the "funner"!

The younger the athlete, the more fun you must create, no matter what the parents think. I've seen a lot of "gung ho" coaches who put together very elaborate and complicated lesson plans for youngsters. They forget that the kids are there to get better and to have fun.

The "winning coach" develops lesson plans that are age-appropriate and incorporates skill development into the fun. Remember, the younger the player, the shorter the attention span. Six-year-olds sometimes have difficulty maintaining focus for more than ten minutes. Use this knowledge to your benefit. Work on technique for 8 to10 minutes and incorporate the skill in a fun game or drill. Afterward, work on a different fundamental for 8 to 10 minutes and then incorporate that skill in a game. Or, you may just want to give them a 10-minute break and play a fun game that has nothing to do with the sport. You can make FUN-damentals fun!

This is true for older children as well. Remember, they are still kids who love having fun. If you get creative and develop drills that they will have fun executing, the kids may not even realize that they are getting better and learning.

# Be positive!
# The best way to teach it is to live it!

The fact is, people like being with and working with people who have a positive attitude. Positive people get sick less, rebound better from difficulties, and are more confident and energetic. People who exhibit a positive attitude typically get better grades, get promotions, are more popular, and become stronger leaders.

Give your players a head start in an increasingly competitive world by demonstrating the positive in all you say and do. It's easy to be positive when things are going your way. The challenge is to be positive in the face of adversity and disappointment. That's when you will have your greatest impact on your kids. How you react after a bad goal, a silly penalty, a missed free throw, or a bad loss will affect your team more permanently than your actions at any other time. During these times, they will watch your behavior and learn how you see the world. Is your world one of anger and excuses? Or, a world of searching for the positives and seeking improvement?

Through example, especially in tough times, rise to the occasion and chart the positive course. Your players will always be grateful.

# Don't focus too much on strategy; focus on skill development.

Many youth coaches spend too much time on strategy. Sometimes coaches are reluctant to teach the fundamentals because they lack athletic talent or are otherwise uncomfortable demonstrating a specific skill. Some veteran coaches simply become bored with teaching the basics and enjoy the "strategy" of the game much more. Of course, we may be able to win a few more games this season with a brilliant strategy that takes advantage of the weaknesses of our opponents, even if our kids can't execute the fundamentals very well.

This focus on strategy clearly undermines the future potential of the athlete and should be avoided at all costs. Great players have a solid grasp of the fundamentals (throwing, hitting, dribbling, passing, blocking, etc.). Working on fundamentals may be a little less glamorous, but it also will give your players the best return on their investment.

Buzz Lagos, head coach of the Minnesota Thunder soccer team, has a passion for the fundamentals. His players can do tricks with a soccer ball that seem physically impossible, and still he insists on his players' perpetual focus on the basics.

I have yet to meet a high school coach who prefers a player that knows a particular "system" of play to one that has outstanding technique, a great heart, strong leadership abilities, and a desire to learn.

Truly outstanding coaches—including high school, college, and professional coaches—see themselves primarily as teachers with a passion for the fundamentals!

# Ensure equitable playing time! Get everyone involved!

Kids join a team to play sports! They do not sign up to sit on the bench. In youth athletics, everybody pays the same amount of money and comes with many of the same expectations. Unless you've got a different type of program in your community than I do in mine, the "superstar" doesn't pay five times more money to participate. So why does he or she get five times more playing time? If you win a game, primarily playing your better players, what did you accomplish? And how do you feel savoring your victory with the knowledge that the other team played everybody equitably? If you win with just your best players, maybe you ought to ask the three or four players on your team who didn't receive equitable playing time if the "win" was worth their sitting out the majority of the game. But you already know the answer to that question.

When youth athletic coaches severely limit playing time for the less talented players in order to win a game, they end up "losing." They lose their integrity as youth coaches. They will probably lose players to a sport because they have effectively communicated to these less talented players that they are no good. Sitting on the bench embarrasses the kids and will surely affect their interest in the game.

I purposely use the word "equitable" versus "equal" playing time because there may be legitimate reasons to vary playing time: different positions involving more or less activity, attendance/behavior issues, health concerns, and so forth. But you simply must go out of your way to make sure that you are fair to every single player on your team.

# Move players around to create success for every player on your team.

Do everything possible to move your players around to different positions during games, especially when players are younger. Don't pigeonhole any player into a spot. The defenseman of today may be the leading scoring forward of tomorrow. The kid you put out in right field today may be the star shortstop tomorrow. Try to give everyone the opportunity to score in a game so that each player has a chance to be the hero at least a few times during the season.

I once had a tall, burly player on a soccer team who moved slowly on the field but had a great attitude. When playing forward during one game, he scored the winning goal! His fellow players almost carried him off the field. I'll never forget the look in his eye. This single split-second moment made his season! And mine, too.

Let every player be a captain during the season. Leading the team in warm-ups before a game and going out there for the coin toss is a big deal! Don't underestimate its importance to the kids! A perfect season is when every single player has been involved in a big play that resulted in a win, and every single player has been involved in a big play that resulted in a loss.

# Concern yourself with the controllables, not the uncontrollables!

At the beginning of the season, I tell my kids and their parents that I will focus on what a player is in a position to control (controllables), not what he or she cannot control (uncontrollables). Controllables are such things as sportsmanship, discipline, listening, effort, and language. Uncontrollables include aspects of the children's abilities or performance, such as netting an easy passing shot, striking out, or making a bad pass.

Sometimes a ten-year-old player may slip on a big play or may lack the speed to be effective on defense. As a coach, you need to remember the child has no control over these incidents. It makes absolutely no sense to waste any energy concentrating on these inevitabilities.

But each player should know that the coaching staff will not tolerate inappropriate behavior, such as putting down teammates, yelling at refs, launching tirades, cursing, and showboating.

When I introduce this concept to my players, it makes sense to them. It clearly communicates how I will respond as a coach. That's the easy part. Now, I have to be in control of my own controllables.

# How you say it is more important than what you say!

Pay special heed to how you talk to children. Always be mindful of who they are and who you are. Keep a positive tone of voice, one void of anger or frustration. Good communication with children begins with a foundation of trust. This trust is built upon the children knowing that you really care for them. Care means that you will give some thought not only to what you will say to them but also to how you will say it.

Think about it. I can say, in a thousand different ways, that one of my players really messed up in a game situation. If I say something in anger or with sarcasm, regardless of the content of the comment, it is hurtful and ineffective. It is ineffective because the child is no longer in a receiving mode, and I have lost an opportunity to help the child learn. But with some thought, I could say the very same thing in a calm, measured voice, perhaps with an arm around a shoulder, in a way that would be constructive, face-saving, and positive. Remember, the goal is to effectively communicate your message and teach your players. When working with kids, you do not have the luxury of blowing off steam.

I have a rule of thumb for communicating with my players: Praise is loud; criticism is quiet. When a player does well, I let everyone know. When a player does not, I attempt to pull the player aside and talk to him or her one-on-one. My exception to this is responding to behavior issues. I will sometimes address these issues in a crowd so that everyone knows the rules will be uniformly and consistently enforced.

# Don't be a bully!

There's no other way to say it. When you yell at a kid just because you can, you are a bully. If your justification for this behavior is "my high school coach yelled at me," it is a poor excuse for a lack of perspective and control. Yelling is simply not a positive tool for modifying behavior.

It's truly shocking to see the way some coaches talk to kids today. It's particularly disconcerting to see the amount of verbal abuse in sports where kids wear helmets. Maybe it's because the kids look older. But Coach, don't forget, there's a kid underneath that helmet! Yelling is demeaning to the player and, quite frankly, to you.

# Caution, parents today are more savvy!

Parents have gotten a whole lot smarter in recent years. They have learned that they don't have to let a coach yell at their kids, like in the old days. Why should they allow you to talk to their child in a way that you wouldn't allow them to talk to your child? Think about it. Would you be offended if another coach talked to your child the way that you are talking to members of your team?

I once overheard a coach yelling at a fourteen-year-old referee, blasting him on his officiating. Very diplomatically, I pulled the coach aside and asked if his kid played hockey and if he thought his son would ever referee when he got older. The coach answered "yes" and "maybe." Then I asked him if he would be angry with a coach who talked to his son the way that he had talked to the young referee. He muttered something and walked away in a huff. But he came back to me ten minutes later and said that he had sought out the adolescent referee and apologized.

Here's a good rule of thumb for coaches: Treat the kids on your team better than you would want another coach to treat your own children! The parents of your players are expecting no less.

# Recognize that different kids have different needs.

Understand that each child on your team has different needs. Some aspire to significantly improve. Others are there more for social reasons. Some are interested in a little of both. Even the most hypercompetitive coach, in more rational moments, has to admit that all aspirations have merit. The "winning coach" keeps this in mind when he works with his team. He may expect greater effort from the more serious player and a little less from the social player. And that is just fine.

Also, be aware that children have different learning styles. Some children learn a skill by seeing others demonstrate it, others by actually doing it themselves. Some need to see it described in writing. And some need to hear about it. I don't expect every coach to become an expert in identifying different learning styles, but if a child is not picking up things as quickly as are others on the team, you may want to experiment with different teaching approaches. If at all possible, customize a coaching strategy and communication style for each child on your team.

# Don't just identify the problem, solve it!

It takes very little skill to criticize a player. "Winning coaches" go beyond the superficial criticism in identifying a problem. They see their role as one of assisting the player with potential solutions.

Here's an example of a tennis coach's evaluation of a high school player: "Erratic. You make entirely too many errors. Your playing time will be dependent upon your consistency." Interesting observation. But other than being too callous and negative, what did this coach offer to help the player improve? Nothing. It took virtually no effort to render these comments.

What could the coach have done? Help the player solve his problems. Specifically, he could suggest that the player try to hit the ball 60 percent as hard to minimize errors, to put more emphasis on and effort into his footwork rather than his arm swing. He could advise the player to be more relaxed and balanced when he strokes the ball.

The point? Any coach can tell a player he or she is doing something wrong. A "winning coach" makes the extra effort to identify the weakness, offers specific suggestions for improvement, and then assists the player to correct the weakness. Yes, it is harder to do. But the rewards are much greater and have an infinitely better chance of helping the player. To paraphrase Jimmy Johnson, the renowned football coach, the difference between an ordinary coach and an extraordinary coach is that little extra!

# Reality check: Videotape yourself.

Do you ever have concerns about your coaching style? Even if you don't, just for the fun of it, have a friend videotape a game or a practice with the emphasis on you. You may be very surprised at the tone you use when you address your players.

Years ago, I asked my wife to tape me. She did so, under the guise of taping my son's soccer game. What did I learn? I discovered that I am a "yapper." My mouth was in constant motion as I coached that team of eight-year-olds. Objectively, 99 percent of the comments were positive, but a couple of times I felt my voice was a little edgy. I also noticed that during halftime my team was more interested in talking to their parents than listening to me.

The tape was a valuable learning tool, and I initiated some changes because of what I saw. I increased the number of "pleases" and "thank-yous" I used when directing kids from the sidelines. I didn't reduce my yapping at the eight-year-olds, but I did consciously try to reduce it as the kids got older. And I moved our halftime meetings away from the parents on the sidelines so that I had more of the kids' attention.

It's a great tool! Go ahead and try it! Remember, early in the season is best.

# Part IV

## Teaching Life Lessons

*When you teach a child, you teach that child's children.*
—The Talmud

# Do what you know is right;
# don't do what you know is wrong.

At the beginning of the year, I tell my players that self-discipline is a must-have quality. In fact, self-discipline may be the single most important ingredient if they wish to succeed in sports, not to mention in life. I give them a very simple definition: you have self-discipline when you do something that you know is right, or when you do not do something that you know is wrong, whether it's easy to do so or not. I finish this talk by stating that you simply cannot become a winner without having self-discipline.

During the season, you will have many opportunities to pull the self-discipline definition out of the bag. Use it when a player takes a bad penalty, swears, criticizes a teammate, or yells at a ref.

# Teach healthy competitiveness.

Competition is good and healthy. Competition is fun. And it's the real world. It is life—relationships, school, work, and sport. No way around it, truly successful people in all walks of life are competitive, and they love being competitive. They are constantly searching for challenge, achievement, and excellence.

Coach Goslin, my high school football and hockey coach, had a significant impact on my development. So much so, that my undergraduate degree was in secondary education and I had hopes of teaching high school and coaching a couple of sports. I learned a great deal from Coach Goslin. But if I had to select the one prevailing lesson he taught me, it would be the pure love of competition. Coach Goslin so thoroughly loved to compete. Not with an "I have to win" mentality, but with a "Gosh, I love to compete" mind-set. His was the purest form of competition that I have ever seen. You could see the love of it in his eyes, whether at a practice or a game. In many ways, it was like he was a kid. He loved being with us and competing with us. Now, I am not saying he didn't love to win, too, but I always had the feeling that winning wasn't what it was about for him. It was the contest.

The battle. Doing your best and accepting the verdict on the field. When you have this kind of mentality, you are a winner the minute you step on the field.

# Encourage intra-competition rather than inter-competition!

When I coach, I like to focus our team on the only thing that we as individuals can control—ourselves, not our opponents. The fact is, in the final analysis, virtually all great athletes, and successful people in general, are competing with themselves first and foremost. When we engage in inter-competition against an opponent, we either win or lose. When we teach our young athletes intra-competition, the concept that they are truly competing against themselves, they can always come out winners, regardless of the scoreboard. Beating an inferior opponent is hollow; losing to a superior rival is meaningless. Walking on the field of competition knowing that you have to better yourself every time you compete, that in every game you play you must execute better than you did the last time, that you must perpetually push yourself to new limits—this is truly a life-altering endeavor. In this way, competition never ends!

I have been preaching this concept for nearly two decades. During my first year of coaching high school tennis, my No. 1 tennis player had the opportunity to play the No. 1

player in the state of Minnesota during a scrimmage. After he lost a lopsided match and shook hands with the superstar, I asked my player how he thought he played in his loss. He was ecstatic! He felt he had played well, with poise, and was proud he had made a number of great points. He couldn't have been more right! Although he was playing the State champ, he was really competing against himself—he looked his personal "demons" in the eye, and he won. That was one of the truly proud moments in my coaching career. I was so proud of him for "winning."

# Emphasize we-play, not me-play.

When coaching a team sport, do everything possible to emphasize we-play. You can't score goals if you don't get assists. You can't score touchdowns if you don't have blocking.

Me-play creeps in when you have players who excel at a sport early. They get all the goals, baskets, or touchdowns in the early days of competition. But when the other children start to catch up, some of these early stars have a difficult time making the transition. Years later they may become challenges for high school coaches. You are not doing these children any favors by allowing them to play selfishly in youth sports.

Another time selfish play surfaces is in a time of crisis: "If we're going to win, I've got to do it all by myself." Sometimes it appears in times of too much success: "It's my turn to score a goal now."

Selfish play, whatever the reason, is clearly counterproductive to team success. Teach your kids to revel in teamwork. I have always loved being on a team. In fact, I've never enjoyed an individual win as much as a team loss.

One of the truly fun things we youth coaches experience is the opportunity to introduce a sports cliché to kids, such as "It isn't over 'til it's over." Or "Give it everything you've got, and then give it some more." Once, I was emphasizing the importance of teamwork between periods of a hockey game. "Gentlemen, we are playing me-hockey instead of we-hockey," and I used the old tried and true, "Remember, there's no I in team!" One of my nine-year-old players looked up at me and said, "Yeah, Coach, but there is an M and an E!" Ya gotta love it!

# Making mistakes is OK.
# Blaming others is not!

Kids, like the rest of us, are going to make mistakes—a lot of them, both on and off the field. We need to teach our kids that making mistakes is an essential part of learning. Blaming others is not. Positively instill in players a sense of accountability and responsibility for their own actions.

As coaches, the first thing we can do is to minimize our reaction to mistakes. Many times, kids seek to extend the blame to others to keep the heat off themselves. But if there's not much heat, then accepting responsibility is easier. Second, we need to make it easy for players to take responsibility by pointing out specifically what happened without assigning guilt for making the mistake. Lastly, we can praise the heck out of the child who looks us in the eye and says he understands, and he will try not to make that mistake again.

Instilling in children a sense of accountability and responsibility for their actions helps them take a giant step on the path to adulthood.

# Teach kids to take chances.

Many times in sports and in life, the risk taker is the winner. If not today, in the future. But in my experience most kids play scared. They are passive when participating in sports because they don't want to get yelled at by their coach, their teammates, or their parents. They think it's better to do nothing than to try to do something—maybe make a mistake, and get yelled at.

I ask my players if they do their best work when they are nervous or uptight about the result. I ask if they feel good when they are anxious about their performance. Not surprisingly, they answer in the negative. It's up to you, Coach. If you are the kind of coach who likes to use fear or intimidation to motivate your players to excel, you are delusional. Don't be the kind of coach that holds his players back because they are scared of how you will react. Youth athletics is all about taking chances and seeing what happens. The person who is too concerned about making a mistake in life is making the biggest mistake of all.

# If you are going to make a mistake, make an active mistake!

If kids are more concerned about making a mistake than making a great play, they will never be great.

I try to make my kids believers in "active" mistakes. Here's my pitch: "If you are going to make a mistake, make an active mistake rather than a passive mistake. If you have a choice of doing something on the field, or sitting back and watching something happen because you're not sure you should, go ahead and do something. Chances are that you are probably making the right play. And if it's not the right play, it's no big deal. It's just a game. I will make you this promise. I will never get mad at you for making active mistakes. Now, I don't want you making the same active mistake three times in a row, but I do want you to be aggressive. That's when you learn the most. That's when you improve the most. And that's when sports are the most fun."

We want to develop athletes who want to push their limits, to see how good they can become. And we coaches must accept, with grace, the consequences of their active mistakes when they do so.

# Coach, you must show respect
# for officials at all times!

The number of incidents involving unacceptable conduct by coaches toward officials seems to increase each year. Coaches, we must do everything we can to curtail this trend. Tell your kids that referees aren't perfect. Officials will make mistakes, just like players and coaches do. We coaches must demonstrate a consistent respect for all authority figures, especially officials. Getting angry and yelling at referees is simply unacceptable. It cannot be tolerated.

Too many times, we give our kids an easy out by blaming the officials. Don't fall victim to this trite excuse. Remember, we are attempting to nurture accountability and responsibility. When we lose, let the kids know that they lost. Perhaps they did not play well, or perhaps they lost to a better team. Most of the time, it's a little of both. But don't let your team off the hook by "blaming the refs." This doesn't build character, it only erodes character.

When you do want to discuss something with an official, try this. Call the official over to a spot away from your players. I do that so the official does not feel intimidated. Then try to put your hand on the official's arm as you talk. Don't raise your voice. It will serve only to alienate the official. Win or lose the discussion, thank the official for coming over. This method has proved quite effective for me, and it's a good opportunity to show the kids how to resolve conflict.

Again, it is impossible to expect our children to respect officials if we coaches do not. Tell your team's parents this goes for them, too.

# Working hard is fun!

Kids need to learn that working hard is fun. As a species, humans were meant to work, to physically and mentally challenge themselves. Have you noticed that truly successful people all love what they do, even though it technically may be defined as work? Working hard in sports can, and usually does, translate into being willing to work hard in other aspects of life—school, long-term relationships, jobs, and life challenges, to name a few.

The best way coaches can teach that hard work is fun is simply to reinforce it during practices and games. Sometimes, we are so exhausted after a task that we don't take the time to enjoy the satisfaction of the effort. Sometimes, we need to be reminded to ask ourselves, "Wasn't that fun?"

Periodically in games and practices, ask your players this question after a workout. Make a big deal about it. Conduct a circuit training drill. After everyone is spent, gather everybody around, compliment all on their efforts, and ask how they feel. You may have to do a little probing, but with a little prompting, players will begin to feel pride in their accomplishments. Usually one or two kids will say, "Boy, that was great! It feels good to work hard." Amen.

# Win like you'd like the other team to win!

At the beginning of each season, I ask my kids how they feel when, after they lose, the other team acts like they just won the Stanley Cup—jumping on each other, screaming, and yelling. They always say they don't like it. Now, I have them set up for the speech: "You're right, it's not much fun to lose to a team like that. So here's what our team is going to do. When we win, we'll act like we'd like the other team to act if they won—with class. Our team will not showboat. We will briefly congratulate our teammates and immediately line up to shake hands with our opponents. We will look each of the opposing players in the eye and say, 'Nice game.' To do any less would detract from our victory."

It is a great lesson for our kids to learn. We bear the responsibility to be gracious in victory, as well as in defeat.

# Learn to lose with class and dignity.

I tell my team that there are only three reasons for a player to get upset after a loss. "First, you can get mad if you didn't give your best effort. Second, you can get upset if you didn't learn anything. Third, you can get upset with yourself if you lost like a loser. If you gave it your best effort, learned something, and lost with class, you really don't have any right to get upset, do you? So, if there is no reason to be upset after we lose a game, we have one more job to do before we can go home: congratulate the winners. We should never detract from our opponent's victory over us by anything less than a winning attitude."

I remember how impressed I was watching the "loser" graciously deal with defeat in truly historic contests: John Newcombe jumping over the net to congratulate Rod Laver, Joe Frazier hugging Muhammad Ali in the ring, Arnold Palmer putting his arm around Jack Nicklaus. In the most visible of surroundings, with incredible personal disappointment, these gentlemen nobly rose to the occasion and sincerely congratulated the winner. This is sport at its very best.

Remember, being a real winner has nothing to do with the scoreboard. It has everything to do with the character of the participants.

# Nurture a "best I can do" attitude!

It's a fact, especially with young kids: they can do only what they can do! When we establish unrealistic goals, we are laying the groundwork for a non-learning experience and one that jeopardizes their affinity for a sport. We need to challenge our players, but not in ways that set them up for failure.

Let's teach our kids to always give it their very best each day. The best they can give you on Thursday may be less than they gave you on Monday. And that's just fine. Your job is to create an environment where they want to give you their best that day. "Winning kids" have a winning attitude, not necessarily a winning record.

# Teach your kids first to be satisfied,
# then never to be satisfied!

You want your players to be satisfied with themselves as players. But you also want to make sure they're always yearning to improve. Much of the joy in life comes from growing. Learning new ways to do things. Attacking more challenging problems. Asking more of yourself in your endeavors. My wonderful eighty-eight-year-old mother-in-law has taught me well. She stays engaged and active, embracing opportunities to learn and grow. That's the true Fountain of Youth. Challenge your kids. Self-improvement is a perpetual process. "Arriving at one goal is the starting point to another," in the words of John Dewey.

# Encourage your kids to think big and dream bigger!

The ability to dream is a wonderful gift. It's important in life for all of us to follow our dreams. In fact, dreams are essential to the development of our children. Help them think big. Is there really any dream that is too big for a child? I hope not. It is better to have kids think big and pull their dreams back in as they grow, than to think small and not reach for the stars when they are young.

Although most players will not become sports superstars, it's not our job as coaches to quash their dreams. Become a champion of their possibilities. Michael Jordan, Joe Montana, Roger Clemens, and Wayne Gretzky were all members of somebody's youth team. Who would have known? Revel in the dreams of your kids and encourage them to reach for the stars!

# Part V

## Winning and Losing

*The moment of victory is much too short to live for that and nothing else.*
—Martina Navratilova

# Chances are, your win/loss record is 80 percent cast before the first game is played.

In youth athletics, your team's record is pretty much determined by who your opponents are, rather than how your team plays. I doubt if many of you coaches out there draft players, or use cash or other perks to attract talent to your team. You are given a group of kids to work with and a schedule to play. If you play weaker teams, you will win. If you play better teams, you will lose. And if you play teams of similar strength you will have close games. Your job as a coach is independent of these facts. Concentrate on improving kids' skills and knowledge.

At the beginning of each season, I tell my kids: "We are going to play some really good teams and some not-so-good teams this year. Our number one goal is individual and team improvement throughout the season. Our goal is to make every game we play better than our last game, and every period we play better than our last period. And I'll tell you what that means in terms of our record this year. It means we are going to win the games that we should win, because we're better than the other team. And it means that we are going to lose the games that we should lose, because we are playing a better team. But our goal should be to win our unfair share of the games with teams of similar talent, because we have worked harder!"

That's really the last time I discuss records with the kids. Whether our record is 8-2 or 2-8 has nothing to do with their talent or worth, and everything to do with the relative quality of their competition.

# Don't think in terms of this season; think in terms of future seasons.

If you are one of those coaches who needs a more tangible measure of success, expand your time horizon. Take a long-term view of your impact as a coach on a group of youngsters. If you feel the need, measure yourself by the wins members of your team experience at older age levels and in high school, years from now, at a much higher caliber of competition. Maybe, that's when you can take pride in the job that you've done.

A few years ago, my oldest son had the pleasure of playing on a team competing for the State of Minnesota High School Boys Soccer Championship. This outstanding group of young men had, in their younger days, been on several teams that experienced average success in competition. Two of the reasons for their success in high school were that they stayed together and they loved the game. But another major reason was the outstanding ensemble of dedicated, positive coaches who worked with them through the years. Every one of these many coaches shared in this team's success during that golden season. All of us took pride in their accomplishments. Yet, we were even more proud of the individuals they had become!

# Be honest and objective when assessing your team!

Too often, coaches associate playing well with winning, and playing poorly with losing. Nothing could be further from the truth in youth athletics. Every team has won playing poorly. Conversely, every team has played well in a loss. But many coaches just can't seem to accept the fact that they lost to a better team; instead, they blame it on the misperception that "we just didn't play well." Some coaches will then seek out reasons for the loss, blaming the effort of one individual or the entire team. From the stands, it's easy to see that the superior team "made" the other team play poorly.

Coach, be honest with yourself and your team. Don't undermine any individual's effort or your entire team's self-esteem because it's difficult for you to admit that your team was just not good enough to win. By the way, that's not an indictment of their value as players or you as a coach. It's just a fact.

"Winning coaches" objectively measure their team, as well as their opponents, and can separate performance on the field from the score on the board. Your team may have lost, playing a great game. Or, they may have won, playing a mediocre game. Remember, good teams do have a way of making less capable teams play poorly. If you lose big time to a better team and you feel your team played poorly, you're probably right. The other team should be commended for making your team look so bad!

My experience is that kids do not take losses as poorly as adults do. But this does not mean that sometimes losses don't hurt young athletes. One of our jobs as coaches is to keep the losses in perspective for our team. One of my favorite sayings after a loss is, "Never let the score tell you how well you played." It takes little effort to identify things that your team has done well during every game. Even in the worst shellacking, you can identify areas of accomplishment. After every game, make sure that you tell your kids how proud of them you are. And always try to compliment the other team to your players. Send the kids over to the cooler for pop and cookies feeling good, wanting to come back and play again.

I coached a soccer team a few years ago for boys nine and under. Our record that year was no wins against ten losses. Nearly every member of that team was either seven or eight years old. A few years later, virtually the same team lost only one league game during the season. Was I proud? Yes, but not of the record. I was proud because virtually every member of that first team had continued to play soccer after that first, what some would call a disappointing, season. The credit for the success goes to the kids and their parents for keeping the season fun, and not dwelling on the losses.

Preoccupation with losses has no place in youth athletics. The number of losses a child experiences in youth athletics is no indicator of future success.

# Don't become a Dr. Jekyll–Mr. Hyde coach!

Beware of becoming a Dr. Jekyll-Mr. Hyde coach. This person during the day is a "good" coach, a Dr. Jekyll, who focuses on the needs of each individual on the team and actually does a pretty good job during practices and during the games the team is winning. But in a close game or on the losing side of a game, he turns into a dark, dastardly coach, a Mr. Hyde, who plays only the best players and berates players and officials alike.

Drama aside, this coach is probably a good person who just lets competitive instincts to win run amok, losing sight of the big picture. But the Jekyll-Hyde coach does a great disservice to the players with the lack of character and inconsistency he or she displays during the game.

# Game suggestion when you're winning big:
## Allow no run-ups, but keep it challenging.

It makes absolutely no sense in a game to run up the score—to embarrass the other team by widening your winning margin to an extreme. Trust me, you will be on the other end one day, and it's not much fun. Running up a score reflects poorly on your program, your team, and you as a coach. But you never want to lose an opportunity to help your players learn. If your kids get way up in a game, set up a game within a game to minimize scoring but maintain learning. For example, you might set up a "dedicated" shooter, determine a minimum number of passes prior to taking a shot, or make up a time of possession objective. And don't forget when the game is over, remind your players to win graciously!

# Blowouts are opportunities to learn and improve.

If your kids get way down in a game, don't give up! Every single game that your team plays is an opportunity for each player to learn and get better. Set new objectives as the game proceeds: "Let's win the last period," "Let's try to shut out the other team for the next few minutes," "Let's score a minimum number of points," "Let's control the ball in their end for most of the period." When you create a new objective, and succeed, you can turn a loss into a big win.

In the midst of an 8-0 blowout, I challenged my soccer team of boys eleven and under to not allow another goal in the last twenty minutes of the game. Guess what! They were successful. "Hey, Coach, we did it! We didn't let the other team score!" The kids were so excited about their accomplishment, even though the other team's coach probably told his team not to score any more goals. No matter, we just turned lemons into lemonade.

In every situation, try to establish a positive, realistic goal that can keep the focus positive and the experience valuable. Never lose an opportunity for your team to learn.

# Losing can be a good thing!

I shouldn't admit this, but a few times in my coaching "career" I looked forward to a loss. Winning against inferior talent is no accomplishment, and actually may be detrimental to the development of young athletes. Sometimes, there is nothing better than a good, old-fashioned walloping by the other team. The fact is, we learn more when we lose than when we win. We analyze a loss more. We work harder because of it. Fortunately or unfortunately, losing is a better motivator. Dealing with adversity, in and of itself, is a growth process. Coach, losing is great when viewed from the right perspective.

# It is about "how you played the game"!

We keep saying, "It's not whether you win or lose, it's how you played the game." If that's so, how come the first thing out of our mouths after one of our kid's games is, "did you win?"

When I coached high school tennis in the late 70s, I could never observe every match because they were played on different courts, often at the same time. Consequently, I made a deal with my team at the beginning of my first season. I promised that, when they had completed a match, I would ask at least two questions before I asked about their score. I would ask them (1) how well they felt they played and (2) if they thought they were improving in the areas we had identified. I would be dying to know their score, but I knew I had to keep my promise by asking at least these two questions. That way I was tangibly reinforcing the emphasis on "how they were playing" rather than on the win or the loss. Both of my teams showed tremendous improvement each year, coming within a couple of points of going to the state tournament in just our second year.

# Part VI

## Tools for Better Coaching

*There are high spots in all of our lives, and most of them come about through the encouragement of someone else.*
—George Adams

# Power is knowledge and confidence!

Get to know as much as you can about your sport! There is a wealth of free information available about every youth sport you can think of. Go to almost any library in the country and you will find shelves of sports material—guides, videos, books, and manuals. There are a great many coaching books that focus on just "your" sport with overviews of teaching technique, overall strategies, the rules, and great drill ideas.

Take advantage of any coaching clinics that are offered. You may learn enough in a three-hour clinic to send you well on your way to a great season! Actually, it's a great way for even the veteran coach to get a head start on the season.

Finally, almost every sport has a monthly or bimonthly publication available to players and coaches. Most of them are free. Seek out these jewels. They typically have great coaching ideas, from organizing and running practices to creative new drills.

Become excited about learning more about your sport. This enthusiasm and knowledge will shine through when you are with the kids.

# Build a positive image
# by making sure you look the part!

Always remember that getting involved in sports is a big deal for kids. Add to the mystique by making sure you look the part. If you are coaching basketball, get the right shorts and look like you're a player. Hockey coaches, don't wear jeans to practice, get a pair of skating pants. Soccer, baseball, and football coaches, buy a pair of cleats. You get the idea. You don't have to go to the most expensive sporting goods store in your city. If fact, worn stuff may have a better impact.

Looking the part extends to the tools of your trade. Buy an inexpensive nylon satchel to carry your lesson plans, team correspondence, player info, insurance forms, game forms, and the like. It can also serve as a mini equipment bag for your whistle, rag, air pump, tape, pens, you name it.

Always have a chalkboard with you. Remember, different kids learn differently. Some need to see it to get it. (Diagramming on the chalkboard also makes you look like a pro!)

Lastly, you must always have a first-aid kit with you. No exceptions! Most community programs will make this available to you without cost. If you must, go out and buy one yourself. It could be the most important investment you make during the entire season. A number of hospitals throughout the country are making these available gratis to youth athletic programs as a promotional device. Check it out. Also, check out a first-aid class for coaches that many hospitals offer.

Remember, the right equipment helps make the coach!

# During the season, periodically go through your coach's checklist.

- Keep things fun and in perspective.
- Be organized.
- Develop a sense of teamwork both on and off the "field."
- Establish objectives and standards for the season.
- Write up lesson plans, every time!
- Keep it SAFE!
- Instill discipline.
- Teach life lessons.
- Balance practices with age-appropriate technique, strategy, and fun.
- Encourage the sport outside of practice and encourage participation in other sports.
- Strive to build a "best you can do" attitude!

# Don't be afraid to get assistance.

The biggest mistake I see us coaches make is not asking for help when we could really use it. Maybe you were the star athlete on your team in the sport that you are coaching and can demonstrate every single technique to perfection. Maybe you understand the game better than anybody else in your community program. But if you are not one of these prodigies, you must ask for help.

With respect to teaching fundamentals, if you don't have either the confidence or the talent to effectively demonstrate technique, you need to enlist a volunteer to do so. Older players in your program, plus high school and college players, are great additions to any youth practice. Most times, the older kids like to come and show off to the younger kids, and I mean that in a nice way. The younger kids absolutely love working with the older kids and actually may develop an increased affinity for the game. Having qualified people teach technique to young players is absolutely mandatory because children (especially the youngest ones) are like monkeys. You do not have to tell them what to do. Just show them, and watch how quickly they pick it up. In my early years of coaching, I did very little bringing in of outside resources. Nowadays, I always try at least a couple of times a season to bring in a "guest lecturer" to run the kids through the paces. It's a great break for me, and for the kids, too.

The same goes for strategy. If you need a little help, ask for it. You will become a better coach!

# Do an end-of-season audit. Run this business by the numbers—the number of "winning kids."

At the end of the season the "winning coach" does an audit. He or she does not look at the win/loss record; that does not tell the story. The "winning coach" takes out a piece of paper and lists the team name at the top and every single player's name underneath. Then, he or she conducts an objective analysis, attempting to assess team progress and the individual growth of each member, both as a player and as a person.

Is the team significantly better today than on the first day of the season? How many individual players made a significant improvement in their skills and knowledge? Did the star player learn to play a more team-oriented style and learn to accept disappointment better? Did the passive player demonstrate more aggressiveness and confidence on the field? What percentage of the team has more self-esteem today than they had at the beginning of the season? How many new friends were made on the team? Did the player who needed the most improvement get the opportunity to make a big play during the season? Did a kid who had a problem with self-control learn to control himself better? Did the team work hard and handle with grace the inevitable ups and downs of the season? Did you, as coach, make the most of opportunities to teach life lessons? These are the important questions to ask, not how many games were won!

When it's all said and done, the only really important statistic to the "winning coach" is the number of "winning kids" he or she helped build.

# In Closing

*Only a life lived for others is the life worthwhile.*
—Albert Einstein

# Remember, it's about the kids!

If you are successful assisting in the development of youngsters, your contribution is infinitely more important than the result of any one youth athletic game, any one youth athletic season. Youth athletic coaches are given a tremendous privilege. We get to hang around kids who are playing a simple game—a kid's game—for a whole season.

Your contest today is just one of literally hundreds of thousands of youth athletic games that take place every day in this country. In the grand scheme of things, winning or losing any single game is inconsequential; being with these children is priceless.

Every single member of your team is a unique individual who deserves the very best nurturing and care—your very best effort to positively impact his or her life. If you are successful in meeting each player's needs, you will become an indelible memory, taken throughout life's journey. If you and others who work with these wonderful children are truly successful, they will become the teachers, coaches, and community volunteers of the future who will carry on the grand tradition of service for their children. What a wonderful legacy!

# About the Author

John L. Shannon, Jr. has been coaching youth athletics for nearly thirty years. For the past fifteen years, John has served as a volunteer coach for more than thirty community youth hockey and soccer programs in Minnesota. He has also served on the boards of various community athletic programs for nearly ten years.

John graduated from the University of Minnesota with a bachelor's degree in secondary education and a master's degree in business administration. In college, he was a member of the varsity tennis teams at St. John's University and the University of Minnesota. John then went on to teach tennis professionally for eight years. As a member of the United States Professional Tennis Association, he worked with young athletes of all ages and abilities. John was a varsity tennis coach at Washburn High School in Minneapolis from 1977 to 1979.

At his day job, John continues to be a coach of sorts, serving since 1989 as president and chief executive officer of successful medical device companies in Minneapolis.

**Please send:**

_____copies of *The Coach's Guide to REAL Winning*

at $ 12.95 each                    TOTAL:            _____

Nebr. residents add 5% sales tax                    _____

Shipping/Handling
$4.00 for first book.
$1.10 for each additional book                      _____

TOTAL ENCLOSED:                                     _____

Name_____

Address_____

City_____State___Zip _____

&#9633;  Visa   &#9633;  MasterCard   &#9633;  American Express

Credit card number _____Expiration date  _____

Order by credit card, personal check or money order. Send to:
Addicus Books Mail Order Dept.
P.O. Box 45327, Omaha, NE 68145
Or, order **TOLL FREE: 800-352-2873**
or online at **www.AddicusBooks.com**